THE HUMAN FIREWALL

Cybersecurity is not ~~just~~ an IT problem

Workshop Edition

Rob May

Our behaviour and the behaviour of the people in our lives (at home and at work) is both the biggest threat and the best line of defence when it comes to cybersecurity. Together we are the Human Firewall, and this was the subject of my TEDx Talk on which the first part of this book is based.

My message is concise, but it's concerning a huge problem that faces us all, I hope that you enjoy what I have to say and that you find it useful.

Stay Safe!

Rob May

The success of my TEDx Talk (which then resulted in both of my short cybersecurity books) is without doubt down to the support that I received from my amazing team at ramsac, my Vistage group (V79) and the unending love and support of my amazing wife.
Thank you to each and every one of you.

The TEDx Talk can be viewed here:
youtu.be/BpdcVfq2dB8

TED promotes "ideas worth spreading"
ted.com
ramsac helps clients to get the best out of technology
ramsac.com
Vistage enables leaders to achieve more
vistage.co.uk
My wife is a legend

CONTENTS

Rob May

YOUR ROYAL WEDDING INVITATION

The social media problem

Social media plays a big part in our daily lives, for many people it is now their primary source of news and social comment. One thing that you can be sure of is that whenever there is a large scale newsworthy event, there will be some form of game or related quiz which you'll be invited to participate in. For example, during the last Royal Wedding I saw such an activity which was to work out your Royal Wedding Invitation Guest Name, you started with either Lord or Lady, then for your first name you use the name of your first pet, your surname is your mother's maiden name, followed by of and your favourite place. I would be Lord Smokey Whitebridge of Chichester (probably).

Due to the usually entertaining results of these games we see them on all forms of social media time and time again. There are many other variants too; during the last UK elections I saw a tweet which detailed how to find your Tory MP name (first name of a grandparent + the name of the first street you lived on hyphenated with your first headteacher's surname).

If you've watched my TEDx Talk you will know that I started my talk with another variant of this game to get their attention. I explained the game and then asked the audience to turn to the person sat next to them and introduce themselves using their resultant alter ego. There was a great deal of laughter and for a moment I was worried I may have lost my audience!

The point of all of these activities (which are supposedly done for fun) is that they trick people into openly sharing information that is frequently used for password retrieval for services such as online banking. During my talk the laughter quickly stopped as it dawned on people the menacing purpose of these social media posts.

Incidentally in the MP name example above, when I saw the post, over 4000 people had replied with their details, I'm sure it continued.

You and I, the people we work with, and our families are being tricked like this all the time and the purpose of this book is to help raise awareness to this and explain how we can prepare and protect.

THERE ARE TWO TYPES OF BUSINESS

According to the FBI...

Two years ago, I was a guest of Microsoft at their UK headquarters in Reading and part of the day included a talk from an FBI Cyber Special Agent. He delivered the message that there are two types of business/organisation: those that have suffered a cyber–attack, and those that will. This is obviously a sobering thought.

During the summer I was again with Microsoft but this time in Toronto, Canada. I'd taken my seat when the same FBI Cyber Special Agent came on to the stage. He started his speech with "There are two types of business" and I thought to myself, 'I've already heard this'. But this time he had a very different message. What he went on to say was "There are two types of business/organisation, those that have suffered a cyber–attack and those that don't know they have!"

This really changes things. We used to believe that the pain of an attack was felt when it happened. What we now understand is that there is no way of knowing when the attack happens. A breach will happen with the explicit criminal purpose of learning about you, your business, your communication paths and styles so that the information can be used against you in some form of cybercrime at some point in the future.

CYBER IS HUGE

The number one crime

To clarify, cybercrime is any form of crime relating to or using computers. Unfortunately, every three seconds someone suffers from identity theft online because of a cybersecurity attack.

It used to be that the international drug trade was the number one form of crime worldwide; that's no longer the case. It is estimated that the cost of cybersecurity worldwide is rising by one trillion dollars a year. In 2017 the cost was four trillion dollars (three trillion GB pounds) and that is expected to continue to rise year on year for the foreseeable future.

It's hard to visualise that much money, but if $4,000,000,000,000 was stacked in one dollar bills it would reach the moon and weigh 40 tonnes (ignoring gravity for a moment!).

Cybersecurity really is a huge problem and it affects every single one of us.

So that being the case, we need to ensure that we are taking appropriate precautions in protecting our lives.

THE HUMAN FIREWALL

The people solution

Most people invest in traditional solutions to protect themselves, they spend money on a hardware or software firewall to prevent unauthorised access to their information technology.

The thing we need to accept is that the biggest risk to our security and also the best form of defence is our people. In the IT industry this is known as the human firewall.

Paying attention to your human firewall is of vital importance.

In my commercial life I have worked with many clients and unfortunately witnessed far too many cybersecurity attacks. There comes a stage in most of these attacks (part of the grief process) where the CEO will call me and say something like "We've taken all your advice, we've purchased an industry leading hardware firewall, we've got anti-virus on all our devices, we pay for email and web filtering, have computer-based training, staff cyber briefings and we've still suffered an attack". My response is always "You've invested wisely and done all you can to protect yourself, but if figuratively your business was a house, what you've done is purchased the very best alarm system, you've put bars on every window and each door has a five-lever mortice lock. You employ security guards at night and staff have had training, but in the instance of most attacks the problem is almost always that a criminal has metaphorically walked up to the front door and pressed the buzzer and a member of the team has let them in."

WHAT IS YOUR DATA SECURITY WORTH?

More than your staff think

Every year there is an event that takes place at Olympia in London called InfoSec. This is a two-day affair for information security and cyber professionals from across Europe, the Middle East and Africa (EMEA) to gather and learn and share all things cybersecurity. I do realise that for many people this sounds like hell on earth but for someone like me it's great!

During the 2016 conference a survey was carried out for research. It took place at Liverpool Street Station which is a busy, London commuter station (it's the third busiest in the UK and connects overground and underground lines coming into the City). Travelers were surveyed during both the morning and evening rush hour periods. They were asked three questions:

1. What is your name?
2. What company do you work for?
3. What is your network password?

Amazingly 34% of people stopped completed the survey – truly shocking! And it got much worse because the people conducting the survey were surrounded by boxes of chocolate Mars bars and if someone refused the survey they were offered a Mars bar in exchange for their participation. In total 70% of the people stopped completed the survey – 70%!

Now the cynic in me believes that some people will have given fake information to get a chocolate bar, but the fact that 34% completed it from the get go makes me think that there would have been a fair amount of actual user data willingly disclosed.

The thing with cybercrime is that it is a numbers game and if this had been a real scam then the criminals would only need some of that information to be true in order to later use it to attack many organisations and individuals.

OUR DIGITAL FOOTPRINTS

The data trail we leave behind

In the rush hour survey example we were dealing with people knowingly (and foolishly) giving away security information. One of the big problems however is that every day many people are unwittingly giving information away.

In the UK there is a fraud prevention service run by Cifas called identityfraud.org.uk, they do a great job educating the public about some of the cyber problems we face. A victim of identity fraud might not realise they've been targeted until a bill arrives for something they didn't buy, or they experience problems with their credit rating. To carry out this kind of fraud successfully, fraudsters usually have access to their victim's personal information which they obtain in a variety of ways such as hacking and data loss, and often using social media to put the pieces of someone's identity together. It is notable that of all the fraudulent applications made for financial products or services during 2016, 88% of them were online submissions.

In my TEDx Talk I showed a clip of a film Cifas produced called 'Data to go', it's a great clip that brilliantly highlights the digital footprints which we all leave all over the web – a huge problem.

In the film what you see is a lady stood outside a coffee shop who is stopping pedestrians asking them to use their mobile phone to 'like' the store's Facebook page in return for a free coffee and a pastry. Parked outside the building is a van which contains a couple of people with laptops connected to the web who can speak to the baristas via discrete ear pieces to give them information. People 'like' the coffee shop's Facebook page and then head inside to collect their reward. In the time that it takes the barista team to brew and deliver their drinks, the van team have trawled Facebook and the web to uncover information about the customers, and the baristas are told the information. They write selected highlights on the side of the coffee cup, i.e. where they work, how old they are, where they studied, names of their children, their faith etc. before handing the cup to the customer. The response of the shoppers is utter bewilderment and whenever I use this clip I get a similar response from the audience.

It's scary stuff but what it should do is make you consider what you're doing online – what are you associating with and attributing your name to? Do you know who these people are and who else might access this information?

GUARDING YOUR DATA

The corporate data pipeline

When I look at any organisation and I consider their security, I visualise it as a pipe. The pipe has lots of junctions and joints and at every one of those there is a person.

When we consider our human firewall the question we need to ask is "Do our people know what they need to do to keep their bit of the pipe secure and stop a data breach happening?"

Please don't think that this can be left to one person either. A single individual cannot effectively maintain your corporate pipe, it must be everyone's responsibility and every person in your organisation needs to be aware of it.

SCAMS CONTINUE TO DEVELOP

We need to talk about them

I'm constantly hearing about scams, some of them quite sophisticated and others not so much, but it always surprises me the reaction I get when I point them out. It is my belief that we need to be openly discussing them, both at work and at home.

A good example of one such scam is known in the industry as the Starbucks scam. I want to point out that this isn't specific to Starbucks and is just as likely to happen in any public place, but Starbucks is so ubiquitous that everyone can relate to it.

The way this scam works is you enter the coffee shop and take out your device, you look for a Wi-Fi connection and near the top of the list is a Wi-Fi network name (SSID) called 'Starbucks Free Wi-Fi', so you connect to it. The issue is that this is not what Starbucks call their Wi-Fi and in fact what you've just done is connect to a criminal who is sat in the corner of the store with his laptop broadcasting a Wi-Fi name. Once you've connected he can scan your device for all sorts of personal information, photos, passwords etc.

Please be careful with what you connect to – whenever I can I always use my phone's 4G connection rather than risking a public Wi-Fi point that I can do nothing to authenticate.

Another is the hotel scam. You check in to a hotel and go to your room. The scammer calls the hotel and asks to be put through to room 136. Reception should announce the call and check to see if you want to take it, but most are too busy, so the call gets put straight through to the room. You answer it and the voice on the end of the line says "Hello, sorry to disturb you, but when you checked in earlier we had a problem with your credit card details please can I take them from you again?". What you should do if you get that call is to say, "That's fine I'll come back down to reception with my card", you certainly shouldn't be reading out your details over the phone.

Now obviously there is a big element of chance here in terms of this scam working as that room may not have just been checked in to, but as we discussed before this is a numbers game and the criminal doesn't need to harvest many credit card details to have had a successful day at work.

I LOVE AFRICA

Phishing for help

I truly do have a big heart for Africa, I think it's an amazing place and I'm blessed to have had many great experiences throughout the continent.

When I'm giving a cybersecurity briefing I usually make the observation that like me you will also no doubt have a long-lost relative who lives there, one whom you didn't know about and now they need your help to get large amounts of money out of their account and in to yours! This type of scam is referred to as phishing and it has been going on since the 1980's, back then it was received by letter or fax and then in the last ten years it's been prolific on email. But despite its 30-year history, people still fall victim to it each and every month.

There are lots of versions of this attack, one I saw recently was sent from a writer who said he was a Director of the state-owned Nigerian National Petroleum Corporation. He wanted to transfer $25 million to the recipient's bank account (money that had been budgeted but never spent). In exchange for transferring the funds out of Nigeria, the recipient would get 30% of the total. To start the process the scammer requested a few sheets of the company's letterhead, bank account numbers, and other personal information.

The long and short of it is that this is an obvious phishing attack and you need to be able to spot them.

WHALING ATTACKS

CEO crime

Phishing has evolved and we've now got what we call whaling. It's so-called because this is a phishing attack aimed at the 'big fish' in an organisation. It is also sometimes called CEO crime.

A whaling attack usually looks like this: An email is received by the accounts department which looks like it's come from the CEO or the Managing Director, giving instructions to move money from one account to another, pay a supplier etc.

You might assume that your team wouldn't fall for this but there is a successful whaling attack every five minutes in the UK.

I was talking to someone at a conference who had been a victim of one of these crimes and she shared her story with me. She was at an exhibition at the time of the attack and she had been tweeting from the venue talking about their stand. The Accounts Manager received an email which he believed was from his CEO and it gave very specific information. The email said "As you know I'm at the show, and last night I met a supplier who is going to help us with Project Kylie. I've engaged his services and I need you to please transfer £7,500 to bank account xxxxx. I'm meeting him for a coffee at 11:00 and I'd be extremely grateful if you could transfer the money before then and give me a call to let me know". The Accounts Manager followed the instructions and phoned his boss to let her know, and when he said, "I've done it" she replied with "You've done what?"

It's worth mentioning that 'Project Kylie' was a secret internal project and only a few people knew about it. I mentioned that the CEO had been tweeting from the show so that piece of the jigsaw was easy. But without doubt this business had been profiled and, as per the FBI story at the beginning of this book, breached a long time before this attack happened. The only good thing in all of this was the criminals only got £7,500, an awful lot less than most of these crimes.

I think the main issue here is culture. When I talk to any organisation who has suffered one of these attacks, invariably the poor person in the accounts department who pressed the button and aided the criminal will say "But the instruction came from the CEO and it's more than my job's worth to not do as I'm told". We need to change the culture in businesses so that it becomes more than someone's job is worth to move money without having a conversation to ensure that the instruction is legitimate, and the CEO really wants it to happen.

EDUCATION

Cybersecurity awareness is a must

In 2017 only one in every five businesses in the UK had any form of formal cybersecurity education. This is perpetuating the problem and I encourage everyone to ensure that in their place of work education and awareness becomes the norm, staff should expect it and all employers should supply it.

Far too many businesses currently justify their lack of cybersecurity training by saying that they have good policies and that these are part of the company handbook which is shared as part of the new employee induction.

An intelligent person needs to hear something six times before they get it and we shouldn't lose sight of the fact that not everyone you work with is intelligent!

On first viewing, this might seem an odd fact but it's most certainly the case. Galileo Galilei famously said, "*You cannot learn anything that you do not know*". This is the reason why you sometimes hear a speaker and think that you've heard the content before, but it is on that occasion that the penny drops and you truly get it.

Harvard conducted a study that showed that when a business person wants to convey an important message they put 85% of their efforts into written word, crafting the right policies or constructing a careful email. Their findings also exposed the fact that only three in every hundred people mentally receive the message being transmitted, they might process it but the meaning doesn't register.

The trouble is we are always processing so much information, there is constant digital noise and copious calls on our attention which means that a single policy document or an email highlighting an issue just won't get through. It's for this reason that you can't rely on simply having a cybersecurity policy – it's just not good enough and it won't achieve what you need.

Remember, an intelligent person needs to hear something six times...

TRUST

It's a difficult subject

Unfortunately, one of the big problems we need to address is that we have to trust less. Yes less! We must talk to our colleagues and educate our children to be sceptical, teach them to be less trusting and question more.

I think that's hard when most of us have grown up in a culture that is essentially trusting. Personally, I've always looked for the good in people and that's part of many people's make-up, but these attacks and scams are quite literally all around us and we must train our thinking and feed the mental computer that our limbic brain takes its guidance from to be far more aware.

If you see an email that sets alarm bells ringing in your head please listen to that inner guide, tune in to your gut feelings. As with most things in life, if something appears to be too good to be true it usually is.

SO, WHAT DO WE DO?

There is hope!

There is hope, and I want to leave you with that message. There are certainly things that we all need to do and basic conversations that are requisite.

Far too many people believe that cybersecurity is an IT problem, but I implore you to accept that it's not. It is something that affects every single one of us, but each of us can have an impact and mitigate the risk, we all need to share the burden of the problem.

I lead boardroom cybersecurity workshops, educating the people at the very top of organisations in just what the issues are and how to prepare for the day when they suffer a breach (remember it's a case of when, not if). These are enlightened leaders and their training makes it so much easier to then spread the message to every person at every level working within the establishment.

We also need to embrace training and education at every level in our schools, our universities and our organisations. Training can be in classrooms and in boardrooms, and it can be delivered electronically. It's really important that everybody takes part in this learning.

I would also urge you to ensure that this is regular and ongoing training. Doing something once, listening to a speaker or attending a one-off course does not reprogram your brain. Don't forget, we need to hear something six times on average before we get it and, in the meantime, new scams are constantly surfacing.

Your human firewall is without doubt the thing that will give you protection from the people element of attacks. You have the power to build that human firewall, and I encourage you to build it high, build it strong and as a result stay safe.

KEY POINTS

Summarising the ideas

This book is designed to be an easy to access primer on the vast subject of cybersecurity, it's aimed at anyone who uses a phone, tablet or a computer, who connects to Wi-Fi or has a social media account. It's based on my TEDx Talk which in itself is a 16-minute key point rundown of a topic I often deliver in a half day workshop. The point is that it's not exhaustive, but it should act as an easily accessible eyeopener which incites important conversation in your home and office.

The key points to remember are as follows:

- Games and 'fun' quizzes on social media platforms often have a sinister purpose.
- There are two types of business: those that have suffered a breach and those that don't know they have.
- Cybercrime is now the number one crime and the cost is rising by $1trn per annum.
- People whilst being our number one risk are also our best form of defence.

- Staff don't value your data security as much as you do and can be bought for as little as a chocolate bar.
- Our digital footprint is vast, and we must think about what we're 'liking' and associating ourselves with online.
- Everyone needs to be instructed on how to look after their bit of your metaphorical corporate pipe.
- An intelligent person needs to hear something six times before they get it.
- You can't learn anything you don't know.
- Don't rely on written words and policies to protect you.
- Scams come in lots of forms and can be stemmed if we'd only talk more about them.
- The person that needs your help to transfer $6m into your bank account is phishing.
- Change your culture so that no one would dream of following an email instruction to move money. Verbal confirmation is a must (regardless of who is giving the instruction).
- Invest in regular ongoing cyber education - staff briefings, Director workshops and computer-based training and testing.
- Trust less, be more questioning and more sceptical (and teach the people in your life to do the same).
- Tune into your gut feelings and listen out for alarm bells in your head.
- Build your human firewall, build it high and build it strong.
- Stay safe!

WORKSHOP NOTES

This section of the book is for the
attendees of
The Human Firewall Workshop

Please use the following pages to take notes and record your action points. By reviewing these key ideas within 24 hours you will increase your recall 200-300 per cent.

TalkTalk
£400k

BIBLE SOCIETY
£100k

UBER
£900k (£385 ICO) v £17m

NAHT
FOR LEADERS, FOR LEARNERS
£50k

_____

_____

_____

_____

_____

_____

_____

_____

_____

_____

ramsac
at the heart of IT

15 Day Hack
380,000 Payments
75,000 passengers
stranded
726 flights
cancelled over 3
days

4% of global
turnover,
2017 BA's total
revenue was
£12.2 billion
Fine circa £500
million

British Airways – fine?

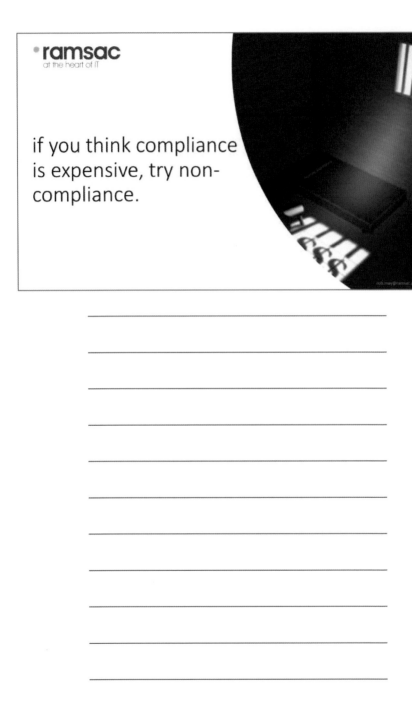

if you think compliance is expensive, try non-compliance.

_____

_____

_____

_____

_____

_____

_____

_____

_____

_____

ramsac
at the heart of IT

your royal wedding guest name

Lord or Lady
First - Grandparent name
Surname - First pet
of
Street you grew up on

Just for fun ...

ramsac
at the heart of IT

15 Day Hack
380,000 Payments
75,000 passengers
stranded
726 flights
cancelled over 3
days

4% of global
turnover,
2017 BA's total
revenue was
£12.2 billion
Fine circa £500
million

British Airways – fine?

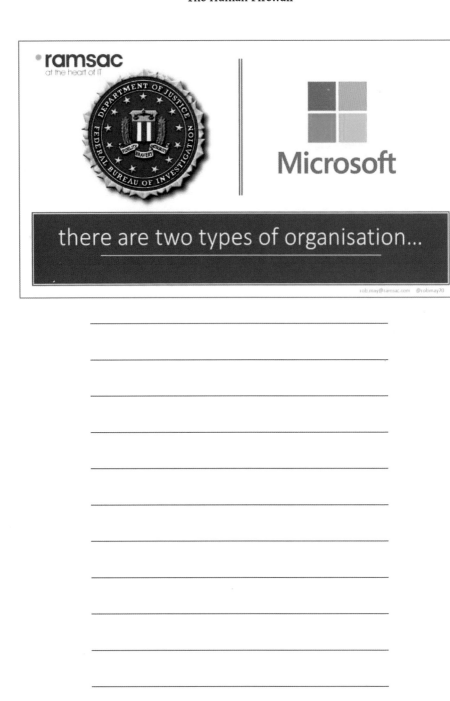

_____

_____

_____

_____

_____

_____

_____

_____

_____

ramsac
at the heart of IT

How do you
educate?

rob.may...ramsac.com   @robmay70

MAL-icious soft-WARE

_____

_____

_____

_____

_____

_____

_____

_____

_____

_____

trust and
scepticism
are part
of the
answer

what's your
password
policy?

_____

_____

_____

_____

_____

_____

_____

_____

_____

_____

the top 25
passwords in
the UK

1. 123456
2. 123456789
3. qwerty
4. 12345678
5. 111111
6. 1234567890
7. 1234567
8. password
9. 123123
10. 987654321
11. qwertyuiop
12. mynoob
13. 123321
14. 666666
15. 18atcskd2w
16. 7777777
17. 1q2w3e4r
18. 654321
19. 555555
20. 3rjs1la7qe
21. google
22. 1q2w3e4r5t
23. 123qwe
24. zxcvbnm
25. 1q2w3e

IDIOT OUTSIDE

ramsac passwords should be like underwear

please change them regularly

don't leave them lying around the office

don't let anyone else use yours

use complex
passwords

_____

_____

_____

_____

_____

_____

_____

_____

_____

_____

whatever you do,
don't buy one of
these!

ramsac
at the heart of IT

LastPass···|

personally I use
LastPass
(the NCSC agree)

this is for you →

1 month *Complimentary Free Premium Trial*
https://lastpass.com/f?41486472

Don't forget
physical security

_____

_____

_____

_____

_____

_____

_____

_____

_____

_____

phishing,
whaling
and
ceo crime

_____

_____

_____

_____

_____

_____

_____

_____

_____

_____

the pay rise
or brexit
scams

_____

_____

_____

_____

_____

_____

_____

_____

_____

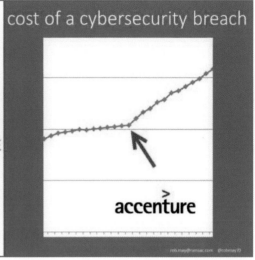

ramsac
at the heart of IT

the cybersecurity threat gap

the gap between investments in:

- Technology
- People
- Processes

MIND THE GAP

_____

_____

_____

_____

_____

_____

_____

_____

_____

_____

_____

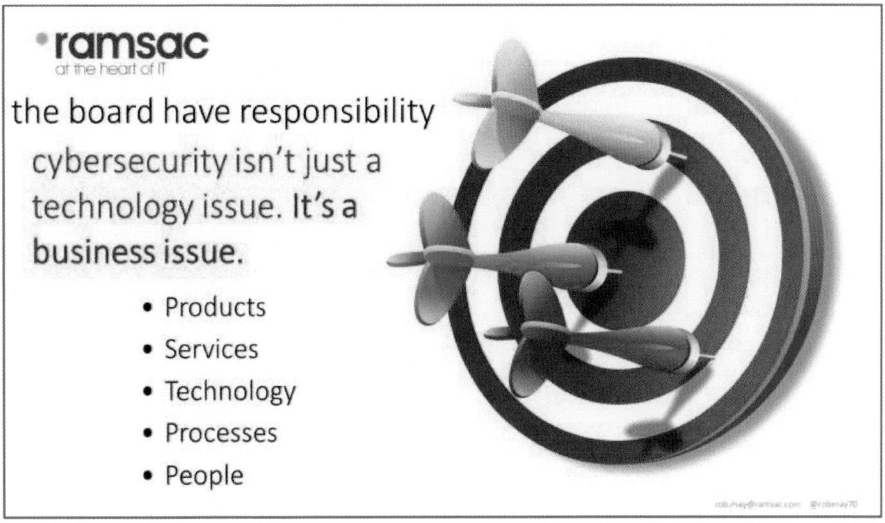

ramsac
at the heart of IT

the board have responsibility
cybersecurity isn't just a
technology issue. It's a
business issue.

- Products
- Services
- Technology
- Processes
- People

•ramsac
at the heart of IT

pwc

Annual Global CEO Survey

60% ranked cyber
threats as top threat to
their growth

what is the state of your
cyber readiness?

_____

_____

_____

_____

_____

_____

_____

_____

_____

_____

_____

9 questions for your next board meeting

Protection of key information assets is critical:

1. How confident are we that our company's most important information is being properly managed and is safe from cyber threats?

2. Are we clear that the Board are likely to be key targets?

3. Do we have a full and accurate picture of:

   i.   the impact on our company's reputation?

   ii.   the impact on the business?

Who might compromise our information?

4. Do we receive regular information from IT on who may be targeting our company, their methods and their motivations?

5. Do we encourage our technical staff to enter information-sharing exchanges with other companies to learn from others and help identify emerging threats?

6. Are all staff receiving on-going regular cybersecurity training and awareness?

Pro-active management of the cyber risk at board level is critical.

7. Are we confident we've identified our key information assets and thoroughly assessed their vulnerability to attack?

8. Has responsibility for the cyber risk has been allocated appropriately? Is it on the risk register?

9. Do we have a written information security policy in place, which is championed by us and supported through regular staff training? Does the entire workforce understand and follow it?

ramsac
at the heart of IT

9 steps to avoid ransomware

1. update O/S and antivirus
2. backup regularly (recovery!!)
3. disable macros
4. beware of malicious emails
5. enable system protection/file history
6. disable Remote Desktop
7. two factor authentication
8. safe protected/known connection
9. avoid questionable web sites

do you have a cyber incident response plan?

PwC Report 2016 – 6000 CEO respondents

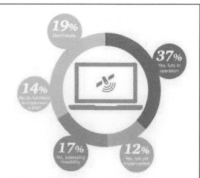

"If you are the leader of a business, you should know how strong your company's defences are, you should know if there are response plans in place in case a significant security breach occurs, and you should be getting regular reports on cyber security threats and what your company is doing to respond to those threats." Jacob Lew, U.S. Secretary of the Treasury, July 2014

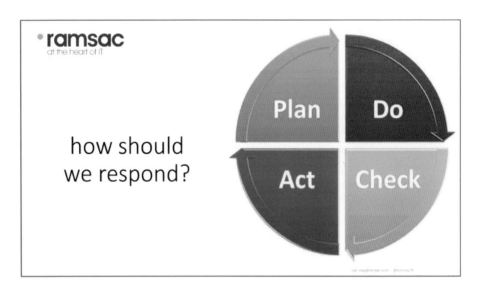

_____

_____

_____

_____

_____

_____

_____

_____

_____

_____

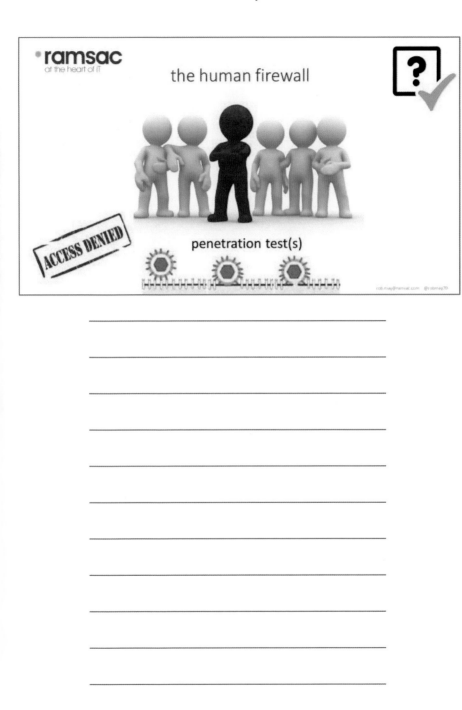

be your
own
solution

_____

_____

_____

_____

_____

_____

_____

_____

_____

the S.O.C.I.A.L. cybersecurity model

S ecurity minded
O rganised
C onscientious
I nquisitive
A ctive
L evel headed

*Repeatedly talk
about the need
to be SOCIAL in
your business*

_____

_____

_____

_____

_____

_____

_____

_____

_____

Your employees have the power

Your organisation relies on your employees, and they are the ones who have the power to make you more or less vulnerable to attacks.

cybersecurity education prevents 40% data breaches

_____

_____

_____

_____

_____

_____

_____

_____

_____

_____

drip feed education

remember, an intelligent
person needs to hear
something 6 times before
they get it...

_____

_____

_____

_____

_____

_____

_____

_____

_____

_____

cybersecurity is an inherent part of the GDPR

GDPR

rights for individuals:

- the right to be informed;
- the right of access;
- the right to rectification;
- the right to erasure;
- the right to restrict processing;
- the right to data portability;
- the right to object; and
- the right not to be subject to automated decision-making including profiling.

ramsac at the heart of IT ICO resources

for the General Data Protection (GDPR) | 12 steps to take now

The ICO has produced a package of tools and resources to help you be compliant. These resources include the following:

- guide to the GDPR;
- GDPR FAQs document;
- advice service helpline for small organisations
- 12 steps to take now infographic.

Links to all of these resources are given to you at the end.

information commissioner's office

0303 123 1113

ramsac
at the heart of IT

GDPR ✓

8 compelling reasons for cyber essentials

It massively helps your GDPR position

It reduces your insurance premiums

It's needed for Public Sector contracts

It prevents approx. 80% of cyber attacks

It increases efficiency and productivity, saving £££

It enhance your organisation's reputation

It can create business opportunities

It shows that you take your clients data seriously

what actions
are you going
to take?

_____

_____

_____

_____

_____

_____

_____

_____

_____

_____

please do feel free to contact me

Thought Provoked

✉ rob.may@ramsac.com

🐦 @robmay70

www.ramsac.com
www.thoughtprovoked.co.uk

📱 mobile: +44 7932 758 522
📞 direct: +44 1483 412 043

_____

_____

_____

_____

_____

_____

_____

_____

_____

_____

_____

_____

_____

_____

_____

_____

_____

_____

_____

_____

Glossary of acronyms and abbreviations

ICO - Information Commissioner's Office

GDPR - General Data Protection Regulation

FBI - Federal Bureau of Investigation

InfoSec – Information Security

NCSC – National Centre for Cyber Security

GCHQ - Government Communications Headquarters

CEO – Chief Executive Officer

O/S – Operating System e.g. Windows

_____

_____

_____

_____

_____

_____

_____

_____

_____

_____

_____

_____

_____

_____

_____

_____

Printed in Poland
by Amazon Fulfillment
Poland Sp. z o.o., Wrocław